Shirley Chisholm
Congresswoman

Written by Garnet Nelson Jackson
Illustrated by Thomas Hudson

MODERN CURRICULUM PRESS

Program Reviewers

Leila Eames, Coordinator of Instruction,
    Chapter 1
    New Orleans Public Schools
    New Orleans, Louisiana

Stephanie Mahan, Teacher
    Bethune Elementary School
    San Diego, California

Thomasina M. Portis, Director
    Multicultural/Values Education
    District of Columbia
     Public Schools
    Washington, D.C.

MODERN CURRICULUM PRESS

13900 Prospect Road, Cleveland, Ohio 44136

A Paramount Publishing Company

Copyright © 1994 Modern Curriculum Press, Inc.

ISBN 0-8136-5241-3 (Reinforced Binding)   0-8136-5247-2 (Paperback)

Library of Congress Catalog Card Number: 93-79428

Dear Readers,

This is a story about a little girl who grew up to be a great American because she cared about others.

Shirley Chisholm was taught early in life to respect herself and her abilities. When she grew up, she spoke out against unfairness, so that all African Americans and women, children, and the poor of all races could also have self-respect.

Let's remember what Shirley believed—that we should fight for the happiness and peace of all.

Your friend,

Garnet Jackson

A ship sailed across miles of blue
water. Waves sparkled in the
sunlight. But four-year-old Shirley
did not like the trip. Traveling on a
ship made her seasick.

1

It was 1928. Her mother, Ruby St. Hill, was taking Shirley and her two sisters, Muriel and Odessa, to a warm island called Barbados. There they would live on their Grandmother Seale's farm.

Shirley was happy when they finally
reached the farm. Their grandmother's
house had many rooms, and many
different animals lived on the farm.

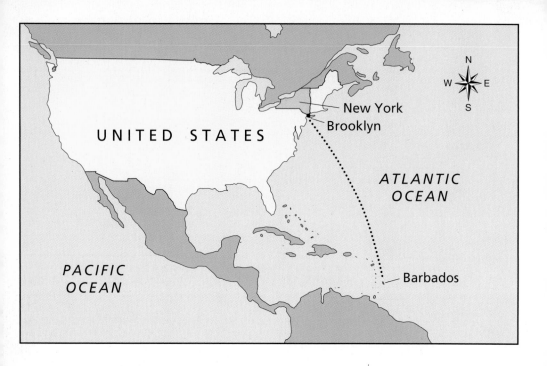

After a short time, Ruby left her daughters and went back to Brooklyn, New York. She and her husband, Charles St. Hill, would work to save money for the girls' education. Shirley and her sisters were sad when their mother left.

Soon the girls began to love the farm. When Shirley started school, she learned quickly. After school, she spent time talking with her grandmother. Grandmother Seale was very loving. With many hugs and kisses, she taught Shirley to be brave and to believe in herself.

The girls stayed on the farm for six years, until Shirley was ten. Then they went back to their parents in Brooklyn. For the first time they saw their new little sister Selma.

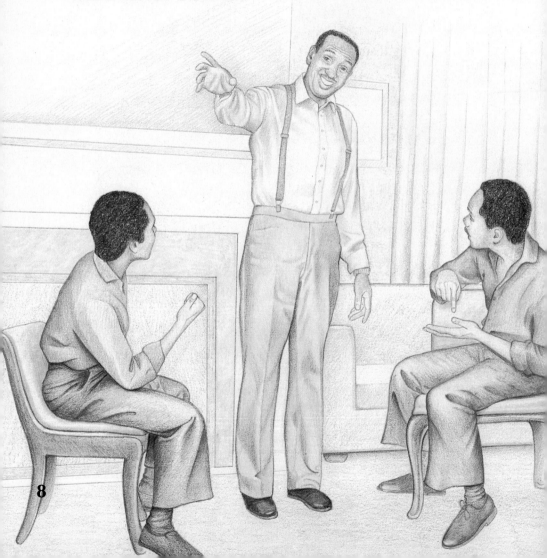

Shirley was smart and did well in school in Brooklyn. She read everything—books, newspapers, and magazines. Shirley also liked to listen to her Dad and his friends talk about the problems of African Americans.

Shirley attended Girls' High School. There she was elected vice president of a club for students with high grades.

She went on to Brooklyn College. Again, Shirley did very well in her classes. She also became known for her strong opinions. She joined groups that talked about ways the government should help people.

11

12

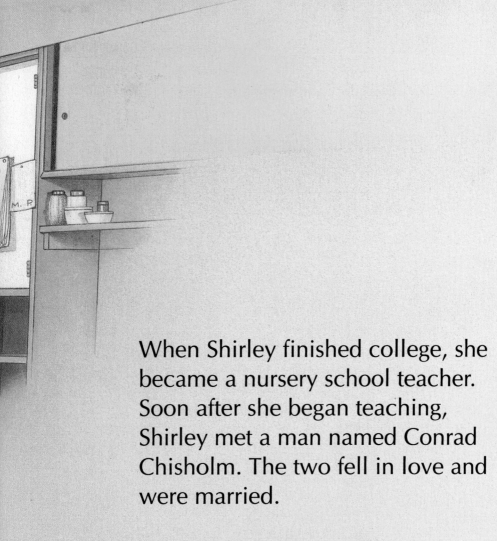

When Shirley finished college, she became a nursery school teacher. Soon after she began teaching, Shirley met a man named Conrad Chisholm. The two fell in love and were married.

For several years, Shirley continued to teach children. But she did not lose her interest in government.

In her free time, Shirley worked with groups that wanted to make government understand the problems of the people. They held meetings and wrote letters to people in government.

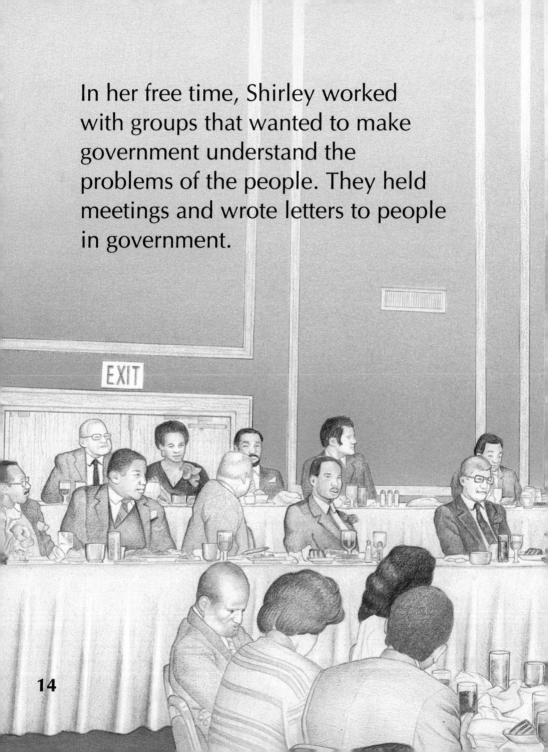

Shirley was a tiny person but she spoke with a big voice. She spoke out especially for new laws to help children, women, African American, and poor people.

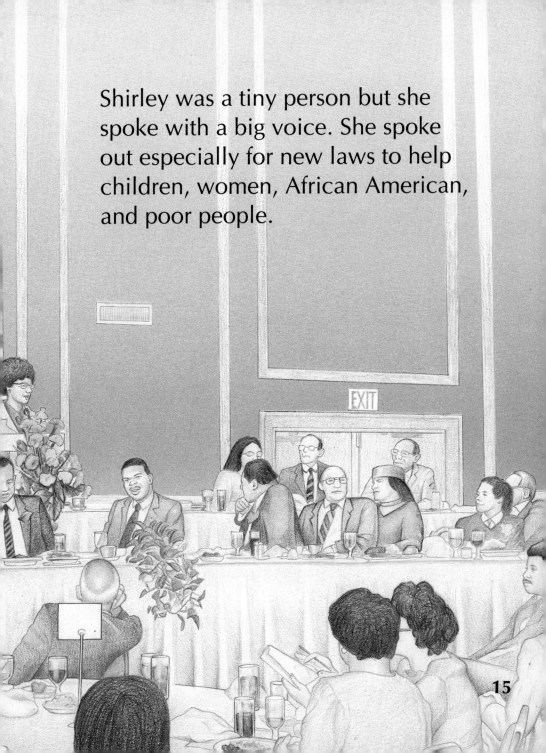

In 1964, Shirley decided to run for the New York State Assembly. Many people thought a woman could not win the election. However, Shirley remembered the words of her grandmother and believed in herself. She talked to the voters face to face. Shirley won the election.

17

In the Assembly, Shirley voted for
new laws. These laws helped women
to get jobs and city neighborhoods to
get youth centers. She became known
as "Fighting Shirley Chisholm."

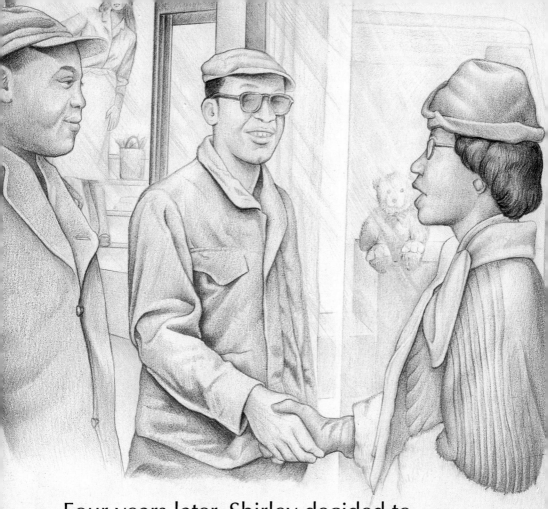

Four years later, Shirley decided to run for the United States Congress. No African American woman had ever been elected to Congress, but Shirley believed in herself. She went from door to door asking people for their votes.

20

21

Shirley won that election, too. She became the first African American woman to serve in the United States Congress.

Many people liked Shirley's ideas. Some told her she should run for President of the United States. In 1972, Shirley was the first woman who had a real chance to try for this office. She showed that both women and African Americans could run for President.

Shirley Chisholm served in the United States Congress for fourteen years, until 1982. She worked to make life better for children, women, the poor, and African Americans. Because she believed in herself, Shirley was strong in helping others.

Glossary

assembly (ə sem′ blē) A group of persons gathered together. In some states, the State Assembly is a group of persons who make laws.

Barbados (bär bā′ dōz *or* bär bā′ dōs) An independent country on an island east of the United States

Brooklyn (brook′ lən) A major section of the city of New York

elect (i lekt′) To choose a leader of a group by having the members of the group vote for one person. The business of voting is called an election. The person who gets the most votes is elected.

government (guv′ ər mənt) All the people and agencies that run or control a city, state, or country

United States Congress (käṅg′ grəs) The branch of government that makes the laws. Congress is made up of the House of Representatives and the Senate.

About the Author

Garnet Jackson was born and raised in New Orleans, Louisiana. She is now an elementary school teacher in Flint, Michigan, with a deep concern for developing a positive self-image in young African American students. After an unsuccessful search for materials on famous African Americans written for early readers, Ms. Jackson produced a series of biographies herself. She has now written a second series. Besides being a teacher, Ms. Jackson is a poet and a newspaper columnist. She dedicates this book with love to her son Damon.

About the Illustrator

Thomas Hudson, a graduate of Cooper School of Art, has worked as a commercial illustrator for nine years and is owner of ILLUSTRATION BOARD. His art work has appeared in *Success Guide* and *Color Me Cleveland*, and in David C. Cook publications. In *Shirley Chisholm*, he uses colored pencil to carry the young reader back into the recent past.